TABLE TALK

## Also by Kevin Ireland

### Poetry

*Face to Face* (Pegasus, 1963)
*Educating the Body* (Caxton, 1967)
*A Letter from Amsterdam* (Amphedesma, 1972)
*Orchids Hummingbirds and Other Poems* (Auckland/Oxford, 1974)
*A Grammar of Dreams* (Wai-te-ata, 1975)
*Literary Cartoons* (Islands/Hurricane, 1978)
*The Dangers of Art* (Cicada, 1980)
*Practice Night in the Drill Hall* (Oxford, 1984)
*The Year of the Comet* (Islands, 1986)
*Selected Poems* (Oxford, 1987)
*Tiberius at the Beehive* (Auckland, 1990)
*Skinning a Fish* (Hazard, 1994)
*Anzac Day* (Hazard, 19970
*Fourteen Reasons for Writing* (Hazard, 2001)
*Walking the Land* (Hazard, 2003)
*Airports and Other Wasted Days* (Hazard, 2007)
*How To Survive The Morning* (Cape Catley, 2008)

### Fiction

*Sleeping with the Angels* (Penguin, 1995)
*Blowing My Top* (Penguin, 1996)
*The Man Who Never Lived* (Random, 1997)
*The Craymore Affair* (Random, 2000)
*Getting Away with It* (Hazard, 2004)
*The Jigsaw Chronicles* (Cape Catley, 2008)

### Non-fiction

*The New Zealand Collection* (Random, 1989)
*Under the Bridge and Over the Moon* (Random, 1998)
*Backwards to Forwards* (Vintage, 2002)
*On Getting Old* (Four Winds, 2005)
*How to Catch a Fish* (Awa Press, 2005)

# TABLE TALK

**KEVIN IRELAND** new poems

Cape Catley Ltd

*For J.*

This book has been published with the assistance of a grant from Creative New Zealand.

First published 2009

Cape Catley Ltd
Ngataringa Road
PO Box 32-622
Devonport, Auckland
New Zealand

Email: cape.catley@xtra.co.nz
Website:www.capecatleybooks.co.nz

Copyright © Kevin Ireland 2009

This book is copyright. Except for the purposes of fair reviewing, no part of this publication (whether it be in any eBook, digital, electronic or traditionally printed format or otherwise) may be reproduced or transmitted in any form or by any means, electronic, digital or mechanical, including CD, DVD, eBook, PDF format, photocopying, recording, or any information storage and retrieval system, including by any means via the internet or World Wide Web, or by any means yet undiscovered, without permission in writing from the publisher. Infringers of copyright render themselves liable to prosecution.

Typeset in Galliard 10/13.5
Designed and typeset by Kate Greenaway, Matakana
Cover design by Trevor Newman, North Shore
Printed by Publishing Press, North Shore
ISBN: 978-1-877340-24-6

# CONTENTS

### PART ONE
*Generalities:*

A new book  9
Sorry about the weather  10
A Greek transaction  11
The man who had great plans  12
A Parnell tale  13
The business side of it  14
Small earthquake in the backblocks  15
Other lives in other books  17
Advice to a young lover  18
The way it all happens  19
Suitable subjects for writers  20
Visitation  21
A view in your window  22
Victory at last  23
Anniversary  25
Waiting for a northern winter  26
A chill on the land  27
Lost page  28
News flash  29
What happens next?  30
Dominion  31
Perfection  32
Losing my lines  33
How to outwit a conspiracy  34
Explaining the past  35
New Year's card for 2009  36
A last visit to Happy Valley  37

PART TWO
*Particulars:*

A letter to the editor  41
Rovrufe  42
Table talk  43
Phrasing you  44
News of the day  45
The poem that defied all reason  46
A new prepositional of love  48
The trouble with emails  49
Local conditions  50
Get my drift?  51
The prospect of travel  52
Snapshot in a city square  53
Istanbul airport  55
Something in the air  56
Paris evening  57
Fine day for love  58
Being rational  59
Phrasal verbs & prepositional phrases  60
On becoming a cohort  61
A taste for words  62
Night talk  63
Joy ride to Albert Road  64
A comic performance  66
What is this thing called love?  68
Vanishing act  69
Word of the day  70
The wish  71
The poem that wrote itself  72
The way things are  73
Writing about you  74

# PART ONE
*Generalities*

# A NEW BOOK

This is the start of a new book.
Which suggest that it's written
back to front. At the very least

it implies that it's a concoction
of thoughts and reports and whatever
with cocked-up connections.

This may not be the best way
to reassure you that its lines are all
that they seem. The best advice

I can offer is that whenever a poet
offers a simple reflection, even with
one hand held sincerely over his heart,

always ask him to turn around,
then prise open his fingers and inspect
what's hidden in his other fist.

# SORRY ABOUT THE WEATHER

Good times are back on Earth again.
The sky has wiped away its tears,
the wind is no longer bashing its head
against brick walls and the rain
has stopped blubbing in the gutters.

It was all set off by something I did
that was wrong. Backsliding gets
the weather it deserves. Everything
was spick and span, then the next day
all hell was let loose. It was my fault.

From now on I am going to behave.
I have no wish to bring the heavens
down around my ears. I no longer have
the nerve. One storm was bad enough,
just spare me the thunderbolts.

## A GREEK TRANSACTION

We were promised there would be
no clouds in July. The breezes would moderate
the heat. The sea would be as blue
as heaven, but deeper. The wine would taste
of spice and pine and summer herbs.
The women would smile and the men
would chop up eggs, cucumbers and tomatoes,
and invite you to be their guest.

Instead it rained for a whole day.
The sea turned a sallow-grey, like putty.
Then the sun was so hot it set fire to the hills,
the wine stripped the enamel off our teeth,
the women turned out to have better things
to do and the men plundered us.

Otherwise it must have lived up
to its best reputation, for our smiles
are glued across our albums. They crease
every photograph as the colours fade
and we wait patiently for the Greeks
to pay up and come to us in their turn
so we can show them what green
actually looks like, what a real mountain is,
how you can lie for hours on a beach
without buying a ticket and what a great time
you can have in paradise
while being eaten alive by sandflies.

# THE MAN WHO HAD GREAT PLANS

It had all been pre-arranged.
There would be sublime weather.
By day the sun would burn off
the clouds and dry up the wind.
At night the moon would ignite
a brand across the waves.

His plans were fixed. No detail
was left to chance. He ticked off
the lists of things that needed
to be done. His world was solid.
It was built with cement and bricks.
He worked at it like a slave.

There was only one thing missing.
He hunted about for it. It had a name
that he could not find. Yet it never
left him alone. At night, in his bed,
in his sleep, it haunted him. He dreamt
on and on of it, to his grave.

*written after a party at Lowry's*

## A PARNELL TALE

*for Bob Dudding*

After that running race I stole
from you and Tony Stones
you joked at least you'd beat me
to the grave. At twenty,
those prophecies seemed funny.

It was our style to pull faces
at the future, and only later
did we realise how close at times
we came to twisting our lips
around whims that were certainties.

Over the decades we would recall
that Sunday morning, after
a Lowry party, waking in your
twin-bunk bach, in Parnell,
nursing our hangovers, sipping tea

and waiting till noon before
we felt well enough to take
a barber's breakfast of a beer
and a roll-your-own then agreeing
how I'd write poems and you'd be

the editor to beat them all.
We raised our glasses and laughed.
At twenty you have no idea
how a freakish notion can freeze
on the wind and shape you forever.

# THE BUSINESS SIDE OF IT

This is the business side of it:
you should aim to give a good account
of yourself and be prepared
(in the cause of striking a balance
that can then be carried forward)
to massage the figures gently
and be creative with your expenditure
and commissions. Always remember
that when you spend up to the hilt
you should make allowance for debts,
dues, discharges and customs,
as well as make acknowledgements
with thanks. And, lastly, never forget
to be had for love not money.

# SMALL EARTHQUAKE IN THE BACKBLOCKS

*for Michael Sharkey*

The prospect from here can be measured
and weighed accurately. It is said to be worth
a fortune, right down to the last dollop of dirt.

Yet last night the earth stifled a yawn
and shook as it rolled over in its bed, and today
I wouldn't trust the look of it. I promise you

that over there you used to see a turned-up nose,
and right beside it stood a huge yet delicate boulder
that could well have been the membrane of a lip.

You would also have picked out arms and thighs,
a shadowed cleft may well have tricked you
into believing in worlds without end,

and you would never have overlooked a shoulder,
a breast and a foot resting against a far horizon.
You will agree with me that landforms go

to enormous trouble to keep copying the parts
of the people who possess title to them.
Real estate quaking with a human face.

Despite last night's disturbance you'll still notice
a hillside of flaking fragments of skin and bone,
and you couldn't possibly miss the beauty of a valley

...

choked with the rubble of broken hearts.
Hard to explain it all, though we try every time
the tectonic plates rattle. And we have one rule,

which is that every new change shall be just like us.
As solid owners of the land we have this duty.
Nothing shall be allowed to spoil our view.

# OTHER LIVES IN OTHER BOOKS

These people are not us. We have never been fictions.
There is no way we would ever have consented
to have our intimacies so poured over and assessed.

It is ludicrous to think we are related to those
who inhabit the pages of books. Their characters
are far too intricate and deep and perfectly expressed.

They can achieve in a few mere strokes of a pen
actions that would take us years to perform.
They can't be more than shadows. They're not real.

Besides, they always dwell on things obsessively
and they don't take time off to sleep or cook or wash.
They are stalked by scruples, yet they can't feel.

We observe their deeds and marvel at their motives,
shake our heads over their moments of indecision
and smile at their invented triumphs and omissions,

yet all they can really do is abbreviate and distort
what we make happen. When we raise our eyes
from the pages of a novel we see apparitions

slink away and conceal themselves behind doors
and curtains. They cannot ever do more than this
for they've no flesh or blood. They're not factual.

Fictions lead entirely other lives. And thank God
for that. Who wants phantoms assuming the form
of terrifying thoughts and daring to be actual?

## ADVICE TO A YOUNG LOVER

Passion is the number one difficulty.
It combusts the brain, firestorms
the spirits, burns the flesh to embers.

My best advice is to stand out for hours
in the rain, or lie in a cold bath, or take
a long swim till at last you remember

why you're doing it. Either that
or take a power-walk in bare feet
over rock and ice, or mud and frost.

The cure won't last long but it sure
will help you clear your mind as you
reckon up your chances and their cost.

# THE WAY IT ALL HAPPENS

There is to be no dancing in the streets today.
Neither shall there be singing, laughing
nor lounging about on park benches.

Also, there is no writing to be done.
All lines, squiggles and loops are banned.
No reason has been put forward for this,

it is simply the new law. Everyone
has been told clearly to lay down their pens
and await further instructions. Already,

stationers, computer shops and publishers
are closing their doors. No one is stupid enough
not to put caution first. They've all heard

the rumour that this is only a trial run
for much bigger things. Pianos, violins
and mouth-organs are next on the list to go.

It is said that people will soon be stopped
from gazing into the sky and there will certainly
be no more kissing. I am writing this only

until the ink runs out. Then I am to join
a happy task force. A brand-new uniform
and a pair of shiny boots come with the job.

# SUITABLE SUBJECTS FOR WRITERS

A list often starts off with the sun.
Yet always the light shuts down at night
just when your poem's begun.

Then there's the wind. Although it puffs
and blusters, just when you need a blast
suddenly there's never enough.

Food and wine are fine, but over the top.
In the market-place of subject matter
they're a bit too much like talking shop.

There's love of course. But poems get on
much better without it. It's tricky stuff.
Something you'd never bet on.

The best subjects are always abstract,
like bliss or beauty. Poems never
go wrong when  they ignore the facts.

# VISITATION

I told myself it could not happen.
No one can plainly, simply disappear.
Yet one moment you were walking

down the stairs and the next
you weren't there. You were holding on
to the rail and you were talking,

then there was silence, or not quite
silence – somewhere a floorboard
creaked and a door closed,

a shadow shifted behind a curtain,
the carpet seemed to rise and fall,
there was a smell of roses.

When later in the day you rang,
you said I must have dreamt it all,
you hadn't been near the place.

Yet I swear it was you all right.
You were wearing a red dress.
It was your body and your face.

There was nothing spooky
about your voice. The tone was calm
and only slightly husky and slow.

But now I cannot tell you what you said.
You made me swear to keep to myself
things that no one must ever know.

# A VIEW IN YOUR WINDOW

The town is torn and trembly in your window.
The bricks no longer build houses but wobble
in the wind like children jostling in a playground,

the sky elbows the chimneys to make room for itself
and the stone lintels make heavy weather of holding
a lid on it all. Slates ripple in scaly radiance, and doors

squirm in the street and muddle up the neighbours.
In the gutters cars cobble together their statements
and shiver, and a dispersal of dustbins declares a shaky

stake in propriety. Passers-by wince and puzzle.
Nerve endings of rails and fences tumble in tangles
and the day is blown away in frenzied shudders.

# VICTORY AT LAST

*Day one:*
After the parade and singing,
the flowers, the champagne,
the kissing of strangers
and the glowing speeches,
and as darkness curses the mess
and the street-sweepers
and the rubbish carts add
a few Amens, it all becomes
like any other victory. A bit
of a let-down really.

*Day two:*
The right side has prevailed
and you can still catch
a vague whiff of hope in the air.
It has even been announced
that a street near the middle of town
will gain a new name.
Yet it is the same old sun
that dusts down the morning
as it rises blearily over the rooftops,
and it is business as usual
as the front door blinks
in the café over the road
and the first customer arrives
for a breakfast of hash,
baked beans and sausages.                ...

Once again, our local road-wreckers
in overalls are holding up the traffic
while they drill out a kerbstone
like a rotten tooth.
Every victory is followed
by a next day.

# ANNIVERSARY

Today is an important anniversary.
Everyone gets a holiday to honour
its significance. Brass bands will play,

and after a grand march past, with floats,
a gun will pound out a salute, then a dignitary
will gloat over us from a balcony.

There will be bunting and streamers,
children will warble and wave flags,
and the day will end with fireworks.

There is always something special
about our celebrations. The last one
was unforgettable, in a misty kind of way.

I recall in particular a young woman
who smiled as she jogged past and raved,
'Anniversaries are fun, okay?'

She must have known she had history
on her side. This is the steamy stuff
that our nation is really founded on.

It was something about her parted lips.
I see them still in dreams. They are red
and moist, like a wound to the heart.

## WAITING FOR A NORTHERN WINTER

Snow is still to come.
The trees aren't bare.
Yet winter's almost here.
They can smell it in the air.

Love has left their sheets.
She combs her hair.
And loss is on the way.
They can breathe it everywhere.

Weather runs their lives.
The tale is old.
The whiff of summer's gone.
Now sniff their bed gone cold.

## A CHILL ON THE LAND

There is sometimes
a chill on the land
that is more than weather,
more than winter,
a cold that quivers
and jangles in the roots
of trees, deep below
the crackling swell
and roll of the hills,
a cold so gripping
that the glimmer of day
frosts over and the wind dies
in its arms with a sigh
and a last shiver.

## LOST PAGE

This is a lost page. It was picked up
by the wind and cast away.
It is only a scrap of paper,
yet it has knocked around
a bit and seen things
it would rather hint at,
experiences it would not care to talk
too much about, though it would never
try to persuade you that it knows
all that the world could throw at it.

Instead you will notice
how it adopts a style
to make up for the libraries
of information it lacks.
For all its scribbled, bruised
and crumpled look, too many blank lines
give it away. Turn it over,
hold it up to the light
and you will still search forever
to find even an impression of a signature.

# NEWS FLASH

There has just been announcement
that those who have dominion over us
are banning the use of a certain word.
No one shall ever be allowed to repeat it.

The message says that there will be
no more ravings and twitterings.
Soon they will shoot all the birds,
and the clanking sound of the moon's

gold bullion spilling over the sea
shall be forbidden. Neither shall there be
hot breezes ghosting gossip to our ears,
and no cloud shall dare fling messages

across the firmament. We shall all
be much better off for this new rule.
The word they have prohibited interferes
with our concentration and does no good

for our health. It is also unseemly,
as well as disruptive and exhausting.
It provokes civil disorder and it makes
men and women (especially) unmanageable.

We shall be happier and better off without it.
And renegades can expect no mercy.
They say those caught using the word
shall be shot full of golden arrows.

## WHAT HAPPENS NEXT?

Day rose from the rooftops
and hurried on down
into the yawning streets,
rubbing sleep from its eyes.

Stay with me, I pleaded.
Yesterday you rushed
into the west before I had time
even to say good morning.

Never do that again, I said.
I was about to declare my love,
then you became midnight
and everyone went home.

What happens next?
That's what I want to know.
The woman I love is fed up
with readjusting her watch.

# DOMINION

Being handed dominion over birds
and beasts is all very well
but there are aspects to the contract
that most of would like to cop out of.

The feeding and watering, for instance,
and the tendering and the bills
for medicine and mending.
Not to mention the bit tagged on

at the end, the bit to do with dying.
An old dog dies and it's not fun
for either of you, and you both know it.
Accountability isn't all it's cracked up to be.

# PERFECTION

Let us celebrate perfection,
without exactly going
into raptures about it.
There's nothing at all wrong
with the notion of excellence
for those who trust in absolutes,
flawless, unfailing and unsurpassable,
but it fits just a little too uncomfortably
into everyday experience and wisdom.

Perfection lacks a sense of scale.
Its grandeur blinds and deafens us.
It is either too hot to handle or too frigid.
So long may we praise the possibility of it
with eyes closed and minds blank,
while we rock slowly backwards
and forwards on our verandahs.
Then later let's raise a glass
to what we can really get a grip on.

## LOSING MY LINES

It is strange how a sore big toe
reduces the size of the known globe
to something smaller than a golfball.

I lie on my back and forget the rewards
and beauties of great works of art.
I admire only the skill of the hand

that stilled the slurp of blood
and stitched back the part that wanted off.
And now the sum of the wisdom

of the ages has come down to a small list
of duties to make a wound clean
and keep a bandage neat. My feet

have become my horizon, a range
of mountains with its tallest peak
capped in frosty white. I cannot utter

the sighs and trills of love. I've lost
my lines. My aching toe beats out
a rhythm like a big bass drum.

## HOW TO OUTWIT A CONSPIRACY

For hours I have had
poems in my head,
yet every time I sit down
with a pad and pen
I've forgotten what they said.

There must be a conspiracy
against them. Notions of them,
even as I speak, are surely
being shot off from the planet
into outer space.
Fogs, I'm dead certain,
are slowly slurping them up
like blotting paper.
I have no doubt also
that oceans are gulping them whole.
And some of them are, quite obviously,
being fed to the wind – which means
that poetry is being eaten alive
by the very air we breathe.

Next time I think up a poem,
if you don't mind,
I'll write it down secretly
at night, under a blanket,
with you on guard, in bed.

# EXPLAINING THE PAST

You lift the past from a musty chest.
Long ago the moths got at it.
You could choke on the dust.

You hold it up this way and that.
Years have rotted or gone missing.
There is no pattern or shape.

You find the scattered threads
of your days no longer weave meanings.
They are knotted with evasions.

Yet in your youth you wore the past
like a cape. You twirled it about you
and struck poses and caught the light.

But now, as you shake it out at night,
its tatters would not even cover
your bare head, let alone the truth.

# NEW YEAR'S CARD FOR 2009

Let us welcome the New Year with silence.
Let us hold our breath and keep still.
Let there be no yammerers, yowlers or yappers.

No one must say a word to break the spell.
No shrugs, no rolling eyeballs, no finger gestures.
May our bells ring without clappers.

All those who lost their life savings
must stand to attention without moving.
And those who took them for a ride

may take only a single step forward
from a high place. All the rest should cease
moaning and take their punishment with pride.

From now on there shall be no excuse
for wittering on about theft, lost opportunities
or plain bad luck. It makes perfect sense

to suffer. It's the way the system works.
Good times are sure to come again some day.
Let us welcome the New Year in silence.

# A LAST VISIT TO HAPPY VALLEY

What really got to us was the willful way
it was done. The farm was ruined. The fences
were down, the paddocks wrecked.
The farmhouse, which once had seemed
a refuge against all harm and drought and storm,
was trashed, its windows stained with tears.

Once this place was Happy Valley. The hills
bristled with trees and grass ran lush along
the flats. A coal range kept the kitchen warm
and a heady smell of cooking drifted
over the land. Dearest, let us never neglect
our love: this place took years to build by hand
with labour that now seems only the wondrous
outcome of a steadfast indolence.

# PART TWO
*Particulars*

# A LETTER TO THE EDITOR

Has anyone else noticed lately
how the world has suddenly changed?
The winds flit round in circles
and the sun is dull and deranged.

Nothing works as it used to.
birds fly backwards in the skies,
our kettle freezes the water
and our camera tells whopping lies.

The mirrors don't show reflections
and the clocks ignore the time.
All tunes have lost their rhythm
and poems won't rhyme.

Has anyone else noticed lately
how pretence is the thing to do,
and the world's last hope is your smile
and only your love holds true?

## ROVRUFE

Who decided on our words?
Who woke up one morning
and gazed over a raised rump,
a swollen shoulder, a breast
and a weed-bed of hair,
and grunted: 'I'll call it love?'

Why not name it: 'Rovrufe'?
It shudders with the thud of certainty.
It has a boom and bark to it.
'I rovrufe you,' would have helped
the rovrufers of this world
get on with serious rovrufing

instead of having this dumpy
love sound getting stuck
like suet pudding in their throats.
And it would have deterred the quitters.
Imagine the vertigo, the terror
of falling out of rovrufe.

# TABLE TALK

This is the way your life changes:
you ask a question over lunch,
between a glance, a smile, a forkful
of Pad Thai and a sip of wine.

The words are unpremeditated,
yet they assert, almost of themselves,
exactly what is required to point
by certain implication and sure sign

the new way ahead and what shall be.
Let us therefore compliment the chef,
extol the suggestibility of lips,
and offer wine whatever else but praise?

Yet when you answered me I knew that
nothing of look or taste mattered quite
as much as unthought sounds, a trick
of language, an accidental phrase.

# PHRASING YOU

You asked me not to exaggerate,
unless I intend to speak in absolutes,
and by saying so explained precisely why

I have felt this way about you. I have seen
exactly what you are getting at. I have spoken
your dialect, picked up the sly values

and each true meaning, the fragrant purpose
of your conjugations, the irresistible
enjoinments of your syllables.

Yet this morning I awoke with the dew
of your kisses on my lips. I savoured it
and thought: this is a delicious extension

of word power I hadn't ever before
taken into account, this is a part
of speech I haven't come across till now.

I am going to have to learn to phrase you
all over again. This is another lingo.
I must learn to speak in a tongue made new.

# NEWS OF THE DAY

Things have always fallen apart. We
strive for unity, yet all our efforts
end in the fractures of history.
Parts of us are always buzzing off
to parts unknown. We live
only partly by participating.

The news-of-the day now informs us
that apartments are parting company
with owners, that partisans are performing
part-exchanges with their consciences,
that new partitions make peaceful
partnerships possible. My only heartfelt part
in this is to ask: Why then dearest
are we so far apart?

# THE POEM THAT DEFIED ALL REASON

This is the poem that refused to be
in the right place at the right time.
It had a mind and a will of its own
and it declined to be here at hand
when I most needed it. Instead,
it sauntered off into an old dictionary
and buried its head in a blur of words
while I looked for it all over town.

And when at last I got on to it
and demanded that it mention things
of great magnitude about the way
you dazzle me, it simply reclined
against the white sheet of this page
and would not stir, no matter
how loudly I roared or whistled at it.

It had been my intention that this poem
would make known the particularities
of my passion for you, but after
a lot of prevarication the most it would
concede was a wink, as if it actually
knew more that I did, then it asked
if I just might have a few cheese biscuits
and a bottle of wine in the cupboard.      ...

There should be corrective institutions
where unruly lines can be put away
for their own good. Or agencies of law
to impose fines or require them
to suffer so many hours or days
of community service. Whatever are you
going to think of me if I can't even
call the shots over my own poems?

# A NEW PREPOSITIONAL OF LOVE

The sun beats down
my heart heats up,
I read the leaves
in a heady cup.

The why has gone,
the where is over.
The signs most favour
loon and lover.

So on I go,
in, out and ever,
with spell and bell
till time is never.

And still as under
or between
I rise in passion
from a dream.

## THE TROUBLE WITH EMAILS

When you wrote that you were
hurrying to get in to the say
I understood at once that what
you didn't mean was that one day
or another you'd be heard.

So when I wrote to tell you
that I am in live I hope you realised
that this was just a slip of the tip
of my finger as it tried
to fond the right word.

## LOCAL CONDITIONS

In Devonport the conditions
for love poems are at last ideal.
Silent mornings open their green palms,
while the sea flicks over the tiny pages
of waves that speak volumes.

In the coffee bars the customers
stir creamy sugared dreams,
while a lone dog crosses the frontier
by the library and flits forever into
the shadow of a lost thought.

When time spares me I shall
feel compelled to write the poem
that has already chosen itself . This may
well be tomorrow when the conditions
will possibly be even more perfect.

# GET MY DRIFT?

Love is the same as it ever was.
You throw yourself out of bed and under
the shower and into your best suit,
polish your shoes, and feel good
for no other reason than style.

Or, at least, that's what you tell them.
Actually though, you just wake
always to find the gold tooth
of desire gnawing the flesh, with stirrings
and thoughts giving tongue.

Get my drift? Being in love
is the same as whenever,
only sometimes infinitely better.
Let them see for themselves, and hope
it's the same, or more so.

# THE PROSPECT OF TRAVEL

I am slowly ambling across the horizon towards you.
Each small movement burns me up, yet I'll get there.
Day after day goes by with little or no advance.
It's like performing exercises in self-improvement.

To gain speed I am jettisoning books, coats and luggage.
Yet time remains my greatest burden and no blade
will sever its grip. It sits on my back and digs in.
Its fingers are cold and they have me by the throat.

Tomorrow they say they'll send a fast aeroplane.
This will whip things along – though why believe it?
Air travel always makes me think I am going backwards.
One day I know I will set off, then land in my past.

There is only one thing that holds me to my aim.
I am in love and so must learn to gamble.
The condition requires that all bets go on one throw.
Tomorrow I'll sit in the clouds and watch the wheel turn.

# SNAPSHOT IN A CITY SQUARE

We are standing in a city square.
Its clock tower has been constructed
in perfectly straight lines and circles.
The angle of the sun provides proof
that it is some time in the early afternoon.
The flagstones, the palm trees and the hand
of the cameraman do not wobble.
Our arms are linked everlastingly.
Every detail is rock solid and all the colours
are correct. Nothing is unaccounted for
or out of place. The whole scene
has been translated from orderly sequences
of numbers in a computer program.
Its certainties conform to a book of rules.

How is it then that your smile
is so mysterious, so flushed
with knowledge of authenticities
that suggest no boundaries
or directives or defining clauses?
Perhaps, somewhere, just out of shot,
you have become aware that the houses
on the hills are melting and bubbling
across the highways, that the walls
of kiosks, shops and office blocks
are slumping like candle-grease  …

and the skies are running down
gutters of sunlight. Your eyes tell me
that soon we may be all that is left
of this old civilisation. So let us
keep smiling. We may well be
the last people on earth
who still have something
to hold on to.

# ISTANBUL AIRPORT

One minute you were there
in the flesh. And the next,
you were assumed into the heavens.

All that was left on the floor
was a scrap of crumpled tissue
with a blot of lipstick the shape

of a seashell. I counted
the thin white creases bedded
between its moisty red ridges.

That's when it got to me.
The inference in membranes
parted in silent farewell.

## SOMETHING IN THE AIR

It all began at midnight
when you could not be there.
The dark was close and heavy,
and I sensed something in the air.
I did not switch the light on,
for there was nothing I would find.
Although it was all around me,
it itched within the mind.

So I reached out to the emptiness
and touched a secret word.
It was not caught in writing,
but something newly heard.
It whispered 'love' within me
and then the moment went
with you not there beside me
to tell me what it meant.

# PARIS EVENING

You are walking down a boulevard.
It is cold and you are wearing a silk scarf.
You are looking for the precise viewpoint
to catch the moon against the steel web
that stitches the sky of Paris together.
Now you are talking. Your friends laugh
as they lean in to the lens of a camera.
I am there, too, but there is no evidence
of my existence, for I am forever framing
you in my eye and fixing this moment.
You all clink glasses, but suddenly there is
so much noise that I cannot hear a word
of what is said. That, also, becomes
lost evidence. Soon, you wave at me.
It is your signal that I must begin writing.
But when I look up you have drifted away.
The empty glasses blink blindly at me.
Everything has become frosted and silent.
It is night and I am holding a snapshot.
You are wearing a silk scarf, smiling.

# FINE DAY FOR LOVE

The air is warm and calm.
The skies are blue today.
But in my bones I have no doubt
that someone's going to pay.

There's no way that we won't
shell out for each joy and perk.
It's nil for nil and bill on bill.
It's the way things work.

Yet disaster never names a price,
nor snow, nor sleet, nor rain.
Despondency and winter nights
charge only strife and pain –

and it costs no more for grief
and defeat and misery –
there's no tag on their efforts,
they're absolutely free.

Love alone is past a price
and all free reckoning.
It charges zilch and everything
when it comes beckoning.

Love's on the house and yet
it puts your vitals to the knife.
It brings a gift of ecstasy
and only asks your life.

# BEING RATIONAL

It is impossible to think of anything
other than you today. Not that I would ever
complain about the matter. I invited
you to make yourself at ease in my brain,
to swing a hammock in my heart.
Instead I hold the weather responsible.

Just look outside at the wind and rain,
the shredded clouds spattered over hill
and paddock, the animals swinging
their backs into the cold, the trees
bending at the knees – leaves and sticks
thrashing through the sky. What else
but try to be rational about my thoughts?
Our climate has a lot to answer for.

# PHRASAL VERBS & PREPOSITIONAL PHRASES

He is 'looking up' a word
in a dictionary. Then, absent-mindedly,
he is 'looking up' the hallway.
He sees her reclining on a sofa.
Instantly, he is distracted
and he finds himself 'looking up'
her skirts. The mesmeric grammar
of same words and unrelated actions
is going to get him into big trouble.
She is soon sure to 'look up'
and catch him at it. Naturally,
he will blame the parts of speech
he was 'looking into'. He is going to say
that it all started over a problem with verbs,
prepositions and phrases. How could he
have possibly guessed at their willingness
to do so many different things at once?
He will tell her that one minute
he was reading a book and the next
he was spooked by the enticements
of words that simply got out of hand.
It is, one way or another, more or less
the main problem with language.

## ON BECOMING A COHORT

I've just learnt, in Webster's Dictionary,
that a cohort, which I knew to be
a company in a Roman legion,
and later any body of troops
or followers or attendants,
can also mean a solitary companion.

That's great news, for I am,
therefore, by definition,
your cohort – I raise you
as my one-off standard. I am
a solo host, a lone army of lovers.
It's a most singular experience.

## A TASTE FOR WORDS

Temerity was the first word
I tasted as I looked into your eyes.
It was flavoured with little flecks
of sugar crusted over a vinegar base.
It had the vague unlikely savour
of pickled peppers or gherkins
and gobs of honeycomb.

Love never loses its impudence –
which was the next word I tested
on my tongue. Its essence was gall
and strawberries coated with chocolate.

When I fell in love with you
I felt the word bite at the back
of my throat. Love feasts lustily
on pure guts and perfect cheek,
the bitter-sweet tang of ambiguity.

# NIGHT TALK

You said goodnight for now
and hushed the telephone
into its cradle. Yet your voice
still echoes inside me. I fumble

at my ribs and touch the sounds
you made. Every cell of my being
is stacked with manuscripts
and notations in a library

of your utterances. Not a letter
falls out of place. Your phrases
tell all. Your merest whisper
will take my lifetime to translate.

# JOY RIDE TO ALBERT ROAD

Tonight, I am afraid,
I shall have to write you a poem
about not writing you a poem.
It is entirely my fault, not yours.

Instead, I shall have to describe
a trip on a bus I caught
this morning when I carried back
my shopping from the supermarket,

for the extraordinary thing was
that, as soon as I got on, everyone
started talking about you. It so
happened that you were the sole topic.

Passengers of all ages, sexes,
types and whatever elaborated
on your beauty, brains, blessedness
and a whole list of amazing extras.

Then someone at the back
shouted out that you were ace
and the whole bus applauded and blasted
into song. For the first time

in my life I just sat there
and listened – until I got out
at my stop on Albert Road
and strolled home to the echo of Alleluias     ...

and hand-bells. I am sorry I cannot
write you a poem. The bus company
promised me that you can present this
as your next ticket.

# A COMIC PERFORMANCE

What's in it for the world?
That's the first question she asks.
Has it got anything going for it
apart from pleasures and risks?

It makes the world safer,
is what I quickly think to say.
It will take your mind off conflict,
and etcetera and so-and-so.

But does it really get things done?
That's the next question she puts.
Does it help clear the mind?
Will it cure distrust and hate?

Oh yes, I'll say it does, I swear.
It's makes for a steadier hand
and eye, and it's a tonic
all round. That's what I've found.

I'm not too sure, she tells me.
I'm swayed one way then another.
Well, why not give it a go, I urge.
It's no weight, no bother.

What is it called? she asks.
I say there's nothing at all to fear,
we can give it any old name
we might care to, or dare.                ...

All right, she agrees,
I'll give it a go just one time
if you describe it out loud. So I do,
and she laughs all the way home.

# WHAT IS THIS THING CALLED LOVE?

*(…a popular song)*

I studied love
and found she faltered,
tricked and tripped
and ever altered.

I dissected love
to a hundred bits
and never again
would the pieces fit.

I asked her why,
she said she swore
by the skin of her teeth
and bloody claw.

But then I looked
into her eyes
and saw that love
tells golden lies.

She hides her truths
in shimmering robes
and hoodwinks those
who dare to probe.

## VANISHING ACT

I lost a poem about you.
There was this mad dash
upstairs for pen and paper,

but before I could get
to my desk, the word picture
fell right out of my head.

So, instead, this is a poem
about how I managed to make
a complete hash of the race.

One minute I was whisking
a white-hot image sizzling
up the stairs, then crash…

it hit the deck like a sprinter
tripping over his own spikes.
The lines lay in splinters.

# WORD OF THE DAY

Today's word delivered by regular email
from Mr Webster to make me feel
I'm in contact with the world is Luddite.

I know its origins and what it means
only too well. I have had it thrown at me.
These days I bear only a very slight

bruise mark from its blow to my cheek,
as well as a tiny scar on my soul. Okay,
I'm hostile to certain kinds of change,

but what I'd like you to know,
Mr Webster, is that I'd willingly break
into your word factory and disarrange

the machinery of your definition
to take account of those who follow
the tradition of their love and demand

that old and crafty rules shall operate.
We hold fast to the one-time ways.
Love shall not alter. It's a last stand.

## THE WISH

She asked me what
I might desire:
her flesh, her mind,
her eyes of fire?

I asked one wish
and one alone:
a kiss, a leaf,
a river stone.

From these I'll build
a wall that's vast,
a roof above
and love that lasts.

# THE POEM THAT WROTE ITSELF

This is the poem that I have been waiting to write.
I have no idea where it is going, there is just
this desire, which grips and shakes the bars of its words,
to break free, eat fire and sip salt spray on the wind.

It is, nevertheless, the limitations that seal in
and preserve the desperate implications of the marks
we make. It is the dilemmas and constrictions
of your life that give you a taste for fire and salt.

So the poem takes shape. Soon, its last words
will stir themselves to rise upwards to link
with the line above and it will lie in its little case
of meanings and be replaced by the poem that follows.

Soon you will get up from your bed and begin
the new day. You will rekindle the embers
of dream and sense the tang of a distant memory.
Somewhere, just beyond remembrance, you know

I am writing to catch the fragrance of your being
in these restless black letters as they twist
across the page. I watch you close the door then walk
down the street and into a new language.

I am learning its first signs. It is going to be hard.
My voice must accommodate a new grammar
and unfamiliar sounds. I must acquire a new word-list
to live with you forever in flames and spindrift.

# THE WAY THINGS ARE

There are two lenses in the mind:
close up and whatever else. For years
I've been watching long distance
and wide angle, bemused by backdrops.

Yet you perceive things truly as they are,
and at last you've taught me how to hold on
to a position and a view without a shaky eye.
In fact, you've shown me how that very I,

which always shouldered forwards at the snap,
falls with a shutter. And suddenly that's not
the shot I thought it was. We all get up again
and smile. And with this focused information,

we drop into each other's arms at last,
and flicker through the years. In the imaginary
of my heart we zoom from make believe
and find in love the framing of our being.

## WRITING ABOUT YOU

It starts here with you
and a first phrase,
then waltzes down the page.

It bends lovingly
at the knees then darts
forward and around.

It does not miss a beat.
It leaves a word to mark
its every point of touch

as it swirls across a stage
inside the heart. Yet it never
makes a sound.